Science
and
Sustainable Energy

Don Nardo

San Diego, CA

© 2018 ReferencePoint Press, Inc.
Printed in the United States

For more information, contact:
ReferencePoint Press, Inc.
PO Box 27779
San Diego, CA 92198
www. ReferencePointPress.com

LIBRARY OF CONGRESS CATALOGING-IN-PUBLICATION DATA

Name: Nardo, Don, 1947– author.
Title: Science and Sustainable Energy/by Don Nardo.
Description: San Diego, CA: ReferencePoint Press, Inc., 2018. | Series:
  Science and Sustainability | Includes bibliographical references and
  index.
Identifiers: LCCN 2017014521 (print) | LCCN 2017022745 (ebook) | ISBN
  9781682822548 (eBook) | ISBN 9781682822531 (hardback)
Subjects: LCSH: Renewable energy sources.
Classification: LCC TJ808 (ebook) | LCC TJ808 .N365 2018 (print) | DDC
  333.79/4--dc23
LC record available at https://lccn.loc.gov/2017014521

CONTENTS

Renewable Energy to Run People's Homes

> **"Diverse sources of renewable energy have the technical potential to provide all the electricity the nation needs many times over."**
>
> —Union of Concerned Scientists
>
> Union of Concerned Scientists, "Benefits of Renewable Energy Use." www.ucsusa.org.

Sustainable energy, also referred to as renewable energy, is a kind of energy that can be used over and over again and will never be depleted. This is because it is self-renewing by its very nature and therefore does not require human intervention to be replenished. Additionally, the use of nonrenewable energy sources such as coal and oil harm the environment, while sustainable energy sources do not.

Perhaps the most familiar example of renewable energy is solar—that is, the energy that comes from Earth's local star, the Sun. The Sun emits enormous amounts of energy in the form of light and heat each and every second. Some of that veritable flood of out-flowing energy encounters and strikes Earth's surface, where it provides warmth, allows plants to grow, and generates other natural cycles on the planet. That incoming solar energy is reliably sustainable for the foreseeable future. This is because our star is expected to continue emitting energy for at least a few billion more years.

Other well-known forms of renewable energy—or renewables, for short—include wind, geothermal (energy from Earth's superhot core), and hydrogen-based energy. Along with solar energy, these renewables have existed throughout Earth's history. Only recently during that period of more than 4 billion years did humans invent science and begin using it to significantly enhance the positive effects of sustainable energy. Scientific advances in the field of energy renewables were particularly marked during the second half of the twentieth century and first decades of the twenty-first.

A Cleaner Environment

Of those numerous recent scientific breakthroughs, some of the most dramatic have been new ways to utilize solar energy in maintaining people's homes. Such advances promise to create solar technology that will produce all the electricity an average house requires. Moreover, generating that electricity in-house, so to speak, puts less strain on the power grid—the large-scale electrical production system that presently serves most American homes. At certain hours and on certain days when electricity use is unusually high, the grid can come under considerable strain trying to keep up.

Scientific advances in solar technology also promise to create and maintain a cleaner environment, including a less-polluted atmosphere. Put simply, the more homes that come to produce all their own electricity, the fewer the grid will have to support. In turn, the grid's need to burn fossil fuels like coal and natural gas to generate electricity will be reduced. In 2015, according to the US Energy Information Administration, 33 percent of the grid's energy was generated by burning coal and another 33 percent from burning natural gas. Solar power accounted for less than 1 percent of the grid's energy-producing sources.

The main reason to reduce the amount of fossil-fuel burning is because this process pollutes the atmosphere. Such burning creates by-products, including carbon dioxide gas and various solid contaminants. Each year huge amounts of those by-products enter the atmosphere. In 2015 alone, burning fossil fuels to create electrical energy unleashed 1.9 billion tons (1.7 billion metric t) of carbon dioxide into the air, which in turn contributed to the ongoing progression of climate change.

Advances in solar energy technology may allow individual homes like this one outfitted with solar panels to produce all the energy the home needs without taxing the power grid.

Futuristic Test Homes in Seattle

The National Renewable Energy Laboratory (NREL) has studied this problem as well as how to solve it through the adoption of various advanced solar energy–producing systems. (Located in Golden, Colorado, the NREL is the only federal lab dedicated to researching and deploying new sustainable energy technologies.) According to NREL experts, homes that use solar technology to generate all of their electricity work far more efficiently than non-solar homes.

Employing such an in-house solar energy system also reduces pressure on the power grid and makes the environment a little cleaner, the NREL found. In addition, going 100 percent solar powered in this manner will save a homeowner a lot of money each year. NREL researcher Dane Christensen states, "We're talking about a home that supports our lifestyles," but "with added comforts and conveniences." Furthermore, "it will be more automated to make good energy decisions for us, helping to direct and guide the user to energy efficiency and cost savings while maintaining those comforts and conveniences."[1]

Demonstrating the efficiency of the newest scientific advances in solar energy has not been confined to the NREL and other research labs. Some commercial developers have already begun to test the new technologies in actual houses in local communities. In 2015 and 2016, for example, Seattle-based Dwell Development built the Lakeview Solar Community in Kirkland, a Seattle suburb. The project consists of four houses—two single-family homes and two duplex units.

Each of these homes was prewired for solar and features a roof containing sunlight-gathering panels carefully placed so as to maximize solar collection. Each house also has state-of-the-art ventilation systems for super-efficient heating and cooling. Moreover, the builders installed extremely well-insulated windows and doors to reduce heat loss and thereby conserve energy. Still another benefit is the installation in each home of an advanced digital monitoring device. It connects and keeps track of all the electrical appliances in the house and indicates the best times of the day to operate them (depending on how much sunlight is striking the roof panels at any given moment). That eliminates most waste and thus adds to the system's efficiency.

As soon as they were up and running, the houses in the Lakeview Solar Community immediately confirmed the worth of the new solar technologies the NREL had been working on. Experts estimate that each year about 2,844 fewer pounds (1,290 kg) of carbon dioxide will be released into the atmosphere for each of the four homes. Therefore, a total of 11,376 fewer pounds (5,160 kg) of that greenhouse gas will be released each year primarily because the Lakeview houses were built from scratch as solar homes. In addition, each Lakeview homeowner will save an estimated $1,100 per year on energy costs.

For a Cleaner, Brighter Future

Christensen and other scientists are aware that a mere four solar homes will not be enough to make a significant dent in the energy-generation problems facing humanity. As NREL communications officer David Glickson points out, "Of course, the results from a single home are small in the big picture of an electrical grid. But when multiplied by many hundreds or thousands of homes on a neighborhood or community scale, the impacts become significant."[2] The long-range solution, he and other experts say, is twofold. First, over time more and more solar homes should be constructed from scratch; second, as many older homes as possible should be retrofitted, or updated, with various efficient solar systems.

The eventual switch from conventional energy sources to solar and other renewables will therefore be a long and large-scale undertaking involving communities everywhere. "Trying to affect the impacts of how we use energy is something that we are all going to need to do together," Christensen asserts. Studies and breakthroughs in the lab are part of that effort, he says. Also vital is observing "neighborhood-scale interactions to see how homes might work together in a community to maximize their efficiency," as in the Lakeview project. Finally, he states, applying this knowledge on an increasingly larger scale will make it possible for society "to manage energy on a sustainable community basis"[3] for a cleaner, brighter future.

CHAPTER ONE

A World Filled with Renewables

> **❝**Huge sources of energy [are] surging around us in nature [and] there was never any doubt about the magnitude of these. The challenge was always in harnessing them so as to meet demand.**❞**
>
> —World Nuclear Association, an organization that promotes understanding of nuclear energy
>
> World Nuclear Association, "Renewable Energy and Electricity." www.world-nuclear.org.

During the second decade of the twenty-first century, humanity as a whole was still obtaining most of its energy from the burning of fossil fuels. Those fuels—coal, petroleum (oil), and natural gas—provide electricity, heat, and air conditioning for homes and businesses. Also, petroleum products—most prominently gasoline—power cars, trucks, trains, and other vehicles.

Although these substances do provide usable, relatively inexpensive energy, they have some serious drawbacks. First, the planet's supplies of them are limited, which means that sooner or later humanity will run out of them. Second, burning fossil fuels pollutes the environment in a number of ways.

Particularly problematic is that the burning of fossil fuels releases carbon dioxide and other so-called greenhouse gases into the atmosphere. Scientists have conclusively shown that these substances are causing the air and oceans to steadily grow warmer. That process, now known as climate change, is already altering climatic and weather patterns around the globe and is expected to cause ocean levels to rise to unacceptable levels in the decades ahead.

Scientists have been studying and monitoring climate change and its effects. They have also been researching alternative energy sources and urging governments, businesses, and the public in general to adopt them as replacements for fossil fuels. In particular, most scientists advocate switching to sustainable, or renewable, forms of energy. The most abundant example is solar energy. Among the others are wind, geothermal (which taps into Earth's inner heat), hydrogen-based (which unleashes the energy stored in hydrogen atoms), biomass (plant-based), and hydroelectric energy (which uses the energy of moving water).

According to the US Energy Information Administration, in 2015 all of these renewables combined provided only about 14 percent of all electricity consumed in the United States. But that situation is already beginning to change. The consensus of scientists is that the sustainable sources represent both the near and far future of energy production and use. Researchers at the US Office of Energy Efficiency and Renewable Energy say that solar, wind, geothermal, and the others "have the potential to strengthen our nation's energy security, improve environmental quality, and contribute to a strong energy economy."[4]

> **WORDS IN CONTEXT**
>
> **hydroelectric**
> Relating to devices and power plants that transform the energy of moving water into electricity.

Early Approaches to Energy Production

Although sustainable energy saw only marginal use in the twentieth century, particularly when compared to fossil fuels, it was not because renewables were largely unknown. Rather, fossil fuels were preferred as large-scale energy sources in large part because they were relatively easy to collect and convert into usable energy. In comparison, the technology needed to employ solar, wind, and some other sustainable sources on the same scale was still lacking. Put simply, the cost of using existing supplies

The majority of automobiles and other vehicles still use petroleum-based fuels, which are not renewable and contribute heavily to environmental pollution.

of coal, oil, and natural gas was less than that of developing new technologies for large-scale use of renewables.

In fact, solar, wind, and a few other sustainable sources have been well known and used on a small scale for thousands of years. The first known use of renewables was a form of biomass conversion through burning. Namely, early humans burned wood and other plant-based materials to create heat and light and to cook. Eventually, people learned to harness another renewable—the wind—by capturing it in sails and thereby powering ships. People in ancient and medieval times also used both wind and moving water to power mills for grinding grain and doing other farm-related work.

Such rudimentary use of these sorts of renewable energy sources remained largely unchanged for many centuries. It was not until the first substantial awakenings of modern science during the eighteenth century that the potential for major advances in the area of energy production arose. These advances did not then occur, however. This was mainly because of the start of the Industrial Revolution, which took place initially in Britain during the middle to late 1700s. The introduction of textile and other kinds of machines in large-scale manufacturing required a great deal of energy; to make the venture economically feasible, that energy had to be as inexpensive as possible.

At the time, with modern science in its infancy, the prospect of developing solar and wind power rapidly and on the huge scale necessary seemed enormously daunting, if not impossible. In contrast, scientists and industrialists pointed out that a much cheaper, as well as seemingly abundant, energy source was readily available. That source was coal. It could be fairly inexpensively mined and then burned to power the machines that were quickly spreading through Britain.

So coal became the first major modern energy source. It powered not only textile mills and other factory machines but also steam engines, which powered railroads, steamships, and boilers in numerous buildings. To meet swiftly rising demand, coal production increased enormously in Britain. The same thing happened somewhat later in the rest of Europe and the United States, which became widely industrialized during the 1800s. As a result, in 1891 the amount of coal used to power industry was forty times larger than it had been during the late 1700s.

Addressing the Drawbacks of Fossil Fuels

During the 1800s another fossil fuel—oil—joined coal as a major source for generating large amounts of power. A number of scientists and inventors of that era worked hard at developing new and more advanced methods of obtaining energy from these fuels. However, there were also scientists who expressed genuine worry about burning coal and oil in such large quantities. First, they pointed out, such burning produced a great deal of smoke, noxious fumes, and solid contaminants. Hundreds of thousands of tons of these industrial by-products entered and polluted the natural environment each year.

Another drawback of burning fossil fuels, concerned scientists said, was that supplies of those substances—while plentiful for the foreseeable future—were limited. What would humanity do, they asked, if natural sources of coal and oil ran out? The answer to that

A nineteenth-century engraving depicts a British coal-mining operation. Coal powered the Industrial Revolution because it was a cheap and abundant source of fuel.

question seemed to be that people might be able to return to more sustainable forms of energy, but on a larger scale than in the past. In 1873 French scientist and inventor Augustine Mouchot asserted,

> The time will arrive when the industry of Europe will cease to find those natural resources, so necessary for it. Petroleum springs and coal mines are not inexhaustible but are rapidly diminishing in many places. Will man, then, return to the power of water and wind? Or will he emigrate where the most powerful source of heat [the sun] sends its rays to all? History will show what will come.[5]

In anticipation of a much more widespread future use of solar power, Mouchot poured much time and money into creating the world's first solar-powered engine. It converted solar energy into mechanical steam power. Mouchot filled a large metal container with water and covered the open section with glass. Exposed to sunlight, the glass trapped heat inside the closed system and caused the water to boil. That process produced steam, which passed through a connecting tube and powered a small steam engine.

Though workable, Mouchot's solar engine generated only a small amount of energy. To make the idea work on a large industrial scale would have required a lot of money for further research and development. To his regret, the earnest inventor was unable to find those funds. All of the investors he approached pointed out that using existing coal and oil was far cheaper and easier.

Nevertheless, Mouchot was not alone among scientists and other leading thinkers of that era to recognize that sunlight had much potential for the future of energy production. In 1885 German inventor and industrialist Werner von Siemens remarked,

> I would say that however great the scientific importance of [solar energy] may be, its practical value will be no less obvious when we reflect that the supply of [sunlight] is both without limit and without cost, and that it will continue to pour down upon us for countless ages after all the coal deposits of the earth have been exhausted and forgotten.[6]

Energy from Wind and Waves

There were also early modern predictions that wind and hydrogen energy would replace the energy produced by fossil fuels. In the early years of the twentieth century British scientist J.B.S. Haldane pointed out that those sources do not pollute the environment. He proposed that his government should pay to install thousands of large windmills. During the times when no wind was blowing, he suggested, scientists could separate hydrogen atoms from oxygen atoms in water and somehow use the hydrogen to produce energy. Haldane was confident that such renewables would steadily come to replace fossil fuels in energy production.

The predictions about future energy needs by Mouchot, von Siemens, Haldane, and other early modern scientists and inventors had certain things in common. They all agreed that exploiting

NEW JOBS COMING IN WIND POWER

Although scientists say that the future is bright for all renewables when it comes to energy production, a number of experts are particularly enthusiastic about the potential of wind power. If it grows at the rate they predict, they say, it will mean many new jobs. A 2017 story on Boston public radio station WBUR points out, "The country's fastest-growing occupation is wind turbine technician, according to the Bureau of Labor Statistics, with numbers expected to more than double over the next decade." Danial Lutat teaches at Iowa Lakes Community College and is an expert in the wind power field. Describing typical jobs in the growing wind power industry, he says, "A wind technician is a person who basically is kind of a jack of all trades. You're maintaining everything from power generation systems to mechanical systems, instrumentation, and communication systems." As for preparing for such jobs, Lutat adds, "a high school grad with a good, solid foundation in algebra and some basic physics is always a plus. You're dealing with everything from mechanical forces to electrical forces, and obviously that requires a good background in algebra, primarily because you're using complex equations to solve those electrical issues when you troubleshoot."

Robin Young, "Wind Turbine Technician Blows Away Competition as Country's Fastest-Growing Job," WBUR, January 31, 2017. www.wbur.org.

energy sources in limited supply, such as coal and oil, could not be sustained forever. They also focused mostly on solar and wind power as the renewable sources most likely to be used widely in the future. In this, they were partly right. Solar and wind power, along with geothermal power and energy from hydrogen, did turn out to be major focuses of scientific research during the twentieth and early twenty-first centuries.

What those pioneering researchers did *not* foresee was that in the twentieth century science would begin to explore a wide range of other sustainable energy sources. One of the more promising areas in this regard was utilizing the energy inherent in the world's seas. Called both ocean energy and marine energy, it takes two principal forms, one of which exploits the huge, inherent power of sea waves.

Scientists were aware that waves contain potentially usable energy at least as early as 1800. But the research required to find ways of tapping that power source were (and remain) extremely expensive, and at the time society saw no pressing need to pursue that avenue. This situation changed radically during the early 1970s. For political and other reasons, the price of Middle Eastern oil, by then a mainstay of Western energy production, suddenly rose sharply. That spurred new scientific research in the United States and elsewhere into alternative energy sources, including sea waves.

The search was on for a practical wave-energy converter, a device that could transform wave energy into usable electricity. The most promising work was done by University of Edinburgh scientist Stephen Salter, who in 1974 invented the so-called Salter's duck, also called the nodding duck. Each duck, one of several that float side by side on the ocean's surface, is a partially hollow, somewhat egg-shaped object, or bobber. Waves strike it head on, causing it to gyrate back and forth. This produces kinetic, or mechanical, energy. To exploit it, an ingenious set of moving parts connect the duck to a generator located below on the ocean floor, which makes the electricity. In theory, wires connected to the generator would transfer that energy to a grid, which in turn would power homes and businesses.

Tidal and Other Hydroelectric Power

Exploiting wave energy in this manner has remained mainly theoretical because world oil prices fell again in the 1980s. In response, the United States and other Western nations drastically slashed funding for wave-energy research. For that reason, this promising technology was never actually implemented on a significant scale.

Somewhat more successful was scientific research into the other primary form of marine energy—tidal energy. Like the wave version, it exploits the kinetic energy of large amounts of moving water. The difference is that sea waves are generated by wind moving across the ocean's surface. In contrast, the gravity of the Earth-Moon system causes the tides, in which entire columns of water move. Researchers proposed that turbines placed in strategic places near the continental coastlines could power generators that would transform the moving water's energy into electricity.

That theory was first put into practice in 1966, when the Rance Tidal Power Station opened in Brittany, France. At peak times of day, the Rance station's twenty-four turbines generate some 240 megawatts (MW) of electricity per day, enough to power about 130,000 homes. That represents roughly .12 percent of France's total electrical demand. Since the Rance facility opened, a few other tidal stations have been constructed globally, most notably South Korea's Sihwa Lake Tidal Power Station. Completed in 2011, it generates 254 MW of electricity daily.

Tidal energy production is a form of hydroelectric power. The word *hydro* means "water," and tidal stations utilize water as their energy source. Much more prevalent are hydroelectric stations that are built beside dams. They work by pumping some of the dam's trapped water into turbines, which, as in the tidal versions,

China's Three Gorges Dam provides power to the largest hydroelectric plant in the world. Hydroelectric stations produce about a sixth of the electricity generated worldwide.

power electrical generators. The largest hydroelectric station in the world is the one attached to the Three Gorges Dam on China's Yangtze River, which opened in 2012. It produces 22,500 MW of electricity per day, almost ninety times as much as the Sihwa Lake station. In 2015 hydroelectric stations of all kinds, located in some 150 countries, together provided about 16.6 percent of the planet's electricity.

Biomass and Biofuels

Another sustainable energy source that scientists poured a fair amount of time and money into during the twentieth century was biomass, derived from living or recently living plants. The simplest approach to using biomass as an energy source, they learned, is to burn it to create heat. In various parts of the world biomass items such as tree branches and stumps, yard clippings, and wood chips are still used to power stoves and furnaces.

Another approach, which is more indirect and complex, is to convert the plant materials into fuel, appropriately called biofuel. This process uses a wide variety of plants, among them corn, soybeans, bamboo, hemp, and palm trees. Particularly effective and popular is sugarcane, which some countries grow in large quantities and convert into the biofuel ethanol. Brazil leads the world in making sugarcane-based ethanol for auto fuel. In 2015

IS NUCLEAR POWER SUSTAINABLE?

In 2015, 20 percent of US electricity was generated by sixty-one nuclear plants situated in thirty states. These facilities use nuclear fission—the splitting of atoms of the radioactive element uranium. The fission process heats up tanks of water to produce steam, which drives turbines that then power electrical generators.

The uranium deposits in the earth's crust that are used to create nuclear power are plentiful, but limited. And once that uranium is used, it is gone forever. For these reasons, some experts contend that nuclear power is not truly sustainable. But what if another, seemingly limitless source of uranium could be found? Toward that end, scientists and engineers are working on ways to extract uranium from seawater. Seawater contains very small amounts of uranium but because 72 percent of the earth is covered in water (and 97 percent of that is salty ocean water) there is, in fact, a potentially enormous amount of uranium to be found in the world's oceans. As science writer James Conca explains, "Uranium mined from normal uranium rock formations and burned in reactors is gone forever. But uranium extracted from seawater is replenished continuously" through naturally occurring processes. If this technology succeeds, nuclear power could become a viable—and sustainable—energy source for many thousands of years to come.

James Conca, "Is Nuclear Power a Renewable or a Sustainable Energy Source?," *Forbes*, March 24, 2016. www.forbes.com.

and 2016, that nation produced a whopping 8 billion gallons (30.2 billion L) of sugarcane ethanol, a product that has been a boon to its economy and way of life. According to the Brazilian Sugarcane Industry Association,

> Brazil has achieved greater energy security thanks to its focused commitment to developing a competitive sugarcane industry and making ethanol a key part of its energy mix. In fact, Brazil has replaced almost 42 percent of its gasoline needs with sugarcane ethanol, making gasoline the alternative fuel in the country. Many observers point to Brazil's experience as a case study for other nations seeking to expand use of renewable fuels.[7]

In stark contrast to Brazil, the United States has not yet chosen to produce large quantities of biofuels. In 2015, for instance, only 1.6 percent of US electricity was generated by biomass in general. In part, this was because of concerns that although biomass is renewable, burning it releases carbon dioxide and other contaminants into the environment. In hopes of overcoming the problem, scientists are presently working on ways to effectively clean the smoke produced in biomass combustion to remove unwanted by-products.

Such research is only a small part of ever-expanding scientific studies of sustainable energy sources and their potential for the future. Among the growing chorus of advocates of renewables are members of the Union of Concerned Scientists (UCS), a group that works to find solutions to major global problems. A spokesperson for the UCS states that the potential of energy from wave, tidal, biomass, geothermal, and particularly solar and wind is huge and waiting to be properly exploited. In the United States alone, he says, "strong winds, sunny skies, plant residues, heat from the earth, and fast-moving water can each provide a vast and constantly replenished energy resource supply. These diverse sources of renewable energy have the technical potential to provide all the electricity the nation needs many times over."[8]

CHAPTER TWO

Harnessing Sunlight's Vast Energies

❝The tremendous growth in the U.S. solar industry is helping to pave the way to a cleaner, more sustainable energy future.❞

—US Department of Energy

US Department of Energy, "Tackling the Hidden Costs of Rooftop Solar." https://energy.gov.

Virtually all scientists agree that of all the sustainable energy forms, solar has the highest potential for future energy production. This is partly because of the enormous quantity of solar radiation that strikes Earth on an ongoing basis. An estimated 173,000 terawatts (trillions of watts) of Sun-generated energy bathes the planet's atmosphere and surface each and every day. That is ten thousand times more energy than all of human civilization uses in a typical day. Put another way, in only seventy-one minutes Earth receives enough solar radiation to power civilization for an entire year.

Also, solar energy is extraordinarily long lasting and reliable. Scientists estimate that the Sun will continue to shine and generate radiation for billions of years to come, which, in human terms, makes sunlight for all intents and purposes eternal and inexhaustible. In addition, solar energy is clean and does not pollute the environment. "The trick, of course," one expert observer points out, "is to harness this vast amount of clean energy."[9]

Inspired by the dream of harnessing sunlight's vast energies, a number of both national and international scientific organizations now strongly advocate vigorously adopting solar technology to meet the world's electrical and other energy needs. A respected leader among these groups is the International Energy Agency (IEA). Its primary goal is to work toward achieving affordable, clean energy solutions for its twenty-nine member nations, including France, the United Kingdom, Germany, and the United States. (By extension, any major successes the group achieves will over time be shared with nonmember countries.) "Solar energy offers a clean, climate-friendly, very abundant and inexhaustible energy resource to mankind," an IEA spokesperson states. "Solar energy in its various forms—solar heat, solar photovoltaics, solar thermal electricity, solar fuels—can make considerable contributions to solving some of the most urgent problems the world now faces: climate change, energy security, and universal access to modern energy services."[10]

Electricity from Light

Particularly prominent in this IEA statement is the mention of several different forms of solar energy technology, including photovoltaic solar and thermal solar, also called concentrated solar. Of these approaches, probably the most widely known, and presently the recipient of the most research funds, is photovoltaic solar. The roots of scientific investigation of the photovoltaic effect lie in the early nineteenth century.

In 1839 French physicist A.E. Becquerel happened on a curious phenomenon while experimenting with coating various metals with acids. He later described "the production of an electric current when two plates of platinum or gold immersed in an acid, neutral, or alkaline solution are exposed in an uneven way to solar radiation."[11] In other words, when sunlight struck Becquerel's acid-coated gold and platinum plates, a tiny amount of electrical energy was created.

A decade after Becquerel's key observation, English surgeon and amateur scientist Alfred Smee coined the term *photovoltaic* to describe the phenomenon. He based it on the Greek root *phos*, meaning "light," and the modern term *volt*, describing certain aspects of electricity. In this way, *photovoltaic* literally means "electric-

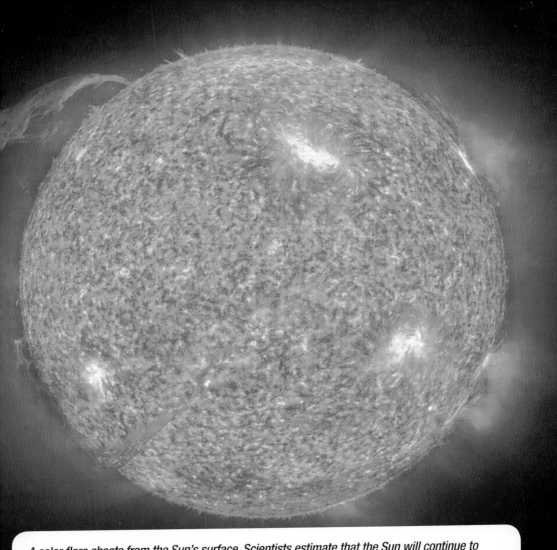

A solar flare shoots from the Sun's surface. Scientists estimate that the Sun will continue to shine for billions of years to come, providing Earth with a virtually eternal source of clean energy.

ity from light." This idea fascinated a number of scientific thinkers. In 1883 American inventor Charles Fritts excitedly predicted, "Solar energy will pour down on us long after we run out of fossil fuel."[12]

One thing that Becquerel, Smee, and Fritts all had in common was that they were unable to explain why sunlight falling on an acid-coated metal surface produced electricity. This was because the existence of the electron was still unknown. In 1897 scientists learned that each atom has tiny units of matter circling its nucleus. They became known as electrons. Meanwhile, inside the nucleus are other tiny units of matter, including protons. Moreover, scientists learned that both electrons and protons carry electrical charges and that electricity is made up of masses of flowing electrons and protons.

During the same era, scientists learned that light is made up of tiny individual packets, or units, which became known as photons (also based on the Greek root *phos*). Knowing these things about atoms and light allowed scientists to finally explain the photovoltaic effect on the surface of a solid metal. Some of the photons of light that fall on that surface strike moving electrons, causing them to enter a higher energy state than they were in before. The result is the creation of electricity.

The Recent Rise of Solar Farms

Over time, scientists learned to obtain increasingly more usable electricity per square inch from an individual photovoltaic surface, or cell. A group of several dozen cells make up a panel. In fact, as research continues, scientists expect that the electrical potential per cell, and therefore per panel, will continue to increase well into the future.

Making photovoltaic cells and panels was at first a very expensive process. As a result, using them to generate enough electricity to power neighborhoods and towns did not begin to be practical until the 1970s and 1980s. The first large-scale solar power facility, often called a solar farm, opened in 1982 near Hesperia, California. Although more such solar farms appeared around the globe in the two decades that followed, they remained expensive to construct. Thus, solar photovoltaic power was not yet a contender in the race to replace fossil fuels with clean, sustainable energy sources.

This situation changed as the cost of making and installing solar cells slowly but steadily came down. The first practical use of solar farms to contribute to a nation's power grid in a measured manner occurred in 2004 when Germany created several hundred such facilities. Most produce more than 1 MW of electricity each day, and more than fifty produce in excess of 10 MW per day. Similarly, by 2008 Spain had installed sixty solar farms producing more than 10 MW per day. Similar solar farms either already exist or are under construction in Italy, India, China, France, Canada, and the United States, among others.

The size of most of these solar photovoltaic farms pales in comparison to a few gigantic versions—frequently called mega solar farms—that opened between 2014 and 2017. Of these, the US national media widely covered the Topaz Solar Farm, which is located near San Luis Obispo, California, and was completed in November 2014. By 2017, Topaz was the fourth-largest solar farm in the world.

SOLAR FARMS AND ENDANGERED ANIMALS

Large solar farms are being built with increasing frequency in countries around the world, including the United States. When possible, they are built on flat pieces of land in remote areas that tend to have few cloudy days in a given year and therefore receive a maximum quantity of sunlight. The southwestern portion of the United States, for example, where the Topaz and Ivanpah solar farms are located, has many areas that fit that profile. Often, getting such a facility off the ground consists of more than just raising the money, buying the land, and beginning construction. As Katie Fehrenbacher, a journalist who specializes in reporting on energy technology, explains, sometimes the types of animals that inhabit that land must be considered:

> Given that large utility-scale solar panel farms like Topaz take up so much land, their potential to disturb environmentally sensitive land is one of the biggest concerns, and obstacles, confronted when creating these types of sites. Other solar sites, like the Mojave Desert solar thermal farm Ivanpah, faced years of delays and protests after initial surveys underestimated the desert tortoises that lived on the land. The main endangered animal living on the land of the Topaz site is the kit fox. To avoid delays and litigation, Topaz's developers purchased extra land for kit fox conservation, and also developed Topaz to be as least intrusive as possible on the surrounding wildlife.

Katie Fehrenbacher, "How the Rise of a Mega-Panel Solar Farm Shows Us the Future of Energy," Gigaom, January 20, 2015. https://gigaom.com.

The cost of the project was high—about $2.5 billion. But supporters point out that the facility will pay for itself over time. It creates roughly 550 MW of electricity per day, enough to power some 160,000 average-size homes. To accomplish this impressive task, Topaz employs panels consisting of thin, chemically coated strips of a combination of the metals cadmium and tellurium.

The farm's daily output of electricity relies less on the metals employed and more on the sheer number of panels. There are a whopping 9 million of them in all, covering about 9.5 square miles (25 sq. km) of mostly arid desert. Katie Fehrenbacher, a journalist who specializes in reporting on energy technology, visited Topaz

Parabolic mirrors that move with the Sun form the basis of the Solar Energy Generating System in Southern California's Mojave Desert. The array of mirrors covers 1,600 acres and generates 354 megawatts of electricity.

in 2015 and was overwhelmed by the enormity of the project. She later wrote,

> From the ground level, looking straight into the solar field is kind of like the fable of the blind man and the elephant. You just can't comprehend the whole picture. For miles in front of me, the millions of panels stretch out across the region, placed in various chunks on both sides of the freeway and strategically positioned around land being used by ranches, homes and a tiny school.[13]

Thermal Solar Power Facilities

Although photovoltaic solar energy is presently the premier version of solar electrical power, science has recently been introducing other kinds of solar energy that are expected to become much more widespread in the near future. One of the more promising is thermal, or concentrated, solar energy. Thermal solar energy uses mirrors or lenses to concentrate a large amount of sunlight onto a relatively tiny spot, which, not surprisingly, becomes extremely hot. That heat powers a turbine, which itself provides the power needed to run a generator that creates the actual electricity.

The key to the overall thermal solar system is the initial concentration, or focusing, of sunlight to produce heat. Scientists have been devising a variety of ways to achieve this step. One that has already seen application in a few commercial solar arrays is a linear concentrator. According to the National Renewable Energy Laboratory (NREL),

WORDS IN CONTEXT

parabolic
Curved.

> Linear concentrator systems collect the sun's energy using long rectangular, curved (U-shaped) mirrors. The mirrors are tilted toward the sun, focusing sunlight on tubes (or receivers) that run the length of the mirrors. The reflected sunlight heats a fluid flowing through the tubes. The hot fluid then is used to boil water in a conventional steam-turbine generator to produce electricity.[14]

In 2017 the largest of the new linear thermal solar systems that had been fully completed was located in San Bernardino County, California. It is called the Solar Energy Generating System, or SEGS. At peak capacity, SEGS creates 354 MW of electricity, which powers tens of thousands of homes and businesses in the surrounding region.

The crucial, cutting-edge core of the SEGS system is its extraordinary array of parabolic (curved) mirrors—936,384 of them in all, covering 1,600 acres (647 ha). If these mirrors were lined up beside one another, the facility's staff points out, they would stretch for 229 miles, or 369 kilometers. One of the most important of the mirrors' features is that each is attached to a guidance system that allows the reflective surface to track the Sun as it moves through the sky each day. That way the mirrors utilize all available sunlight and maintain a high level of efficiency. The only time the system does not operate is at night and on cloudy days.

Another way the still-experimental thermal solar facilities concentrate sunlight is through the use of so-called power towers, or heliostats. Instead of focusing the light on horizontal tubes situated near the mirrors, as in a linear version, the power tower method focuses the sunlight on a small receiver at the top of a tall tower. Fluid inside the receiver heats up and powers a turbine. The world's largest thermal solar facility erected to date—the Ivanpah Solar Electric Generating System, located near Clark Mountain in southern California—utilizes the power tower approach. It actually consists of three separate systems, each with its own heliostat, which work together to create a total of 392 MW of electricity daily.

A thermal solar approach that is even more on science's cutting edge is still in the experimental stages. Its mirrors are encased within a box of solid material that is semitransparent and rests on a rooftop. The mirrors move, aided by a fluid circulated inside the box, and concentrate sunlight on a hot spot in a manner similar

The Ivanpah Solar Electric Generating System near Clark Mountain in Southern California, uses the "power tower" method of concentrating sunlight. Parabolic mirrors focus sunlight onto a receiver at the top of the tower (shown) to heat a fluid to turn electricity-generating turbines.

to the mirrors in the SEGS system. Such a system would be ideal for directly powering a large building like a skyscraper.

Hot Water from Sunlight

Although producing electricity is the most widespread application of solar energy, scientists have also learned to use sunlight for other energy-related purposes. Of these, one of the most critical is providing hot water for homes, businesses, and factories. The basic principle behind solar water heating has been known and used on a small scale since at least 1900.

THE AROUND-THE-WORLD FLIGHT OF *IMPULSE 2*

In addition to producing electricity and heating buildings, solar energy has proven itself useful for powering airplanes. In December 2009, two Swiss men—engineer André Borschberg and balloonist Bertrand Piccard—launched the first fixed-wing aircraft powered only by sunlight. They named it *Impulse 1*. It used a grouping of photovoltaic cells mounted on its wings to power its electric motor. In 2010, *Impulse 1*, with a wingspan of 72 feet (22 m), completed a twenty-six-hour flight from Switzerland to Spain. The solar-powered plane also flew across the United States in 2013.

Hoping to fly such a craft all the way around the globe, Borschberg and Piccard next built *Impulse 2*, which featured more solar cells and a more powerful motor than their first plane. Between August 2015 and July 2016, *Impulse 2* completed a trip around the world in a series of individual legs, or hops, each consisting of thousands of miles. In all, the slow but quiet, efficient, and nonpolluting plane covered about 26,000 miles (42,000 km). Borschberg firmly believes that by improving the technology he and his partner used, solar-powered passenger planes will become commonplace in the near future. "With partners who believed in the same vision," he says, "we developed solutions to make our airplanes very energy efficient. All these technologies can be used today in other applications to make our world more energy efficient as well."

Quoted in Solar Impulse, "André Borschberg, Entrepreneur, Engineer, and Explorer." http://solarimpulse.com.

One of the first and most successful attempts to apply that principle on a larger, community-size scale occurred during the 1950s. Israeli scientist and engineer Levi Yissar designed a workable solar water heater, and in 1953 he established an Israel-based company to manufacture it. Thanks to his efforts, 20 percent of that nation's homes used such devices by 1967. The global crisis surrounding higher oil prices in the early 1970s prompted the Israeli government to require that all new homes be equipped with solar water heaters. In this way, Israel became the world's leader in using solar energy in this manner.

Since that time, tens of thousands of homes and factories in countries around the globe have installed solar water heaters, whose technology is constantly advancing. The newer versions are available in several different forms. In one, a solar collector is placed on the roof. That collector consists of one or more hollow metal tubes enclosed in a box, the top side of which is a sheet of glass. When sunlight passes through the glass, it is trapped inside the box, and in an example of the well-known greenhouse effect, the air inside gets hotter and hotter. Much of that accumulating heat is absorbed by water flowing through the metal tubes. The hot water then passes into a water tank inside the building and from there circulates to pipes in bathrooms, kitchens, and/or workrooms.

Most homeowners who have installed solar water heaters in the past few decades have done so primarily to save money. The NREL, which has studied these devices and their use in detail, points out that it usually takes a minimum of four years for the owner to recoup the costs of installation. After that, the building's hot water is free, and the owner saves hundreds of dollars each year. There can be other benefits as well. According to the NREL,

> Solar water heaters offer long-term benefits that go beyond simple economics. In addition to having free hot water after the system has paid for itself in reduced utility bills, you and your family will be cushioned from future fuel shortages and price increases. You will also be doing your part to reduce this country's dependence on foreign oil.[15]

Passive Solar

Still another way that homes and other structures can benefit from solar energy is through passive solar systems. Here, the term *passive* indicates that no active systems, those involving solar cells, panels, collectors, or other mechanisms, are employed. Instead, the actual living space—the house itself, including its windows, floors, walls, and so forth—acts as a solar collector. Various portions of the residence absorb heat and distribute it to other portions.

The parts of the house or other structure that absorb and temporarily retain the solar heat are collectively called the thermal mass. The primary goal of a passive solar system is to capture and store heat within the thermal mass, which later releases that heat during times of the day when the sun is unavailable. A website maintained by the US Department of Energy (DOE) explains the most common way this works, saying, "Sunlight enters the house through south-facing windows and strikes masonry floors and/or walls, which absorb and store the solar heat. As the room cools during the night, the thermal mass releases heat into the house."[16]

Experts on solar energy say that the key to making a passive solar system work properly and save the structure's owner money over time is to ensure the building is designed correctly in the first place. The DOE cautions,

> Although conceptually simple, a successful passive solar home requires that a number of details and variables come into balance. An experienced designer can use a computer model to simulate the details of a passive solar home in different configurations until the design fits the site as well as the owner's budget, aesthetic [artistic] preferences, and performance requirements.[17]

Even more energy efficient and cost effective are a few recently built cutting-edge homes and other structures like those of the Lakeview Solar Community in Seattle. These futuristic structures combine the passive solar approach with other existing solar approaches, including solar water heating and solar electricity production. Experts on solar energy say that these diverse solar technologies, along with others now in the research stage, hold great promise for meeting future energy needs. "The number of governments at all levels who consider implementing policies to support the development and deployment of solar energy is growing by the day," the IEA states.

> The development of affordable, inexhaustible, and clean solar energy technologies will have huge longer-term benefits. It will increase countries' energy security through reliance on an indigenous, inexhaustible and mostly import-independent resource, enhance sustainability, reduce pollution, lower the costs of mitigating climate change, and keep fossil fuel prices lower than otherwise.[18]

CHAPTER THREE

Clean, Inexpensive Wind Power

> **"Wind power continues to be one of the most promising renewable energy sources. Over the last decade, the wind industry has seen exponential growth, and wind farms are popping up all over the world."**

—Brian Merchant, a reporter who specializes in climate and energy issues

Brian Merchant, "In the Future, Will Wind Turbines Be Everywhere?," HowStuffWorks Science. http://science.howstuffworks.com.

Today one of the most widely used and most promising forms of sustainable energy utilizes the power of the winds that blow through Earth's atmosphere each and every day around the globe. Many people are surprised to learn that wind is an indirect form of solar energy. Sunshine beats down on and heats Earth's atmosphere each day, but that heating process is not uniform. Factors such as the planet's irregular surface features, Earth's constant spinning on its axis, and widespread air pressure differences result in uneven solar heating of the atmosphere. These differences in temperature from one sector of the atmosphere to another set the winds in motion.

Science has revealed that the winds contain huge quantities of kinetic energy. When properly harnessed, that energy can, in theory, provide human civilization with large amounts of clean, relatively inexpensive electricity. Thanks to ongoing scientific advances, today that theory is increasingly becoming a practical reality. The United States, Canada, United Kingdom, Germany,

China, and numerous other nations are progressively pouring money into using wind energy to generate electricity.

The statistics in this regard are telling. In the decade from 2004 to 2014 alone, global wind-powered electrical generation grew from 47 to 369 gigawatts (GW) per day. (1 GW equals 1,000 MW.) At the beginning of 2015, Denmark created 21 percent of its electricity through wind technology, widely acknowledged as an unusually large proportion. That figure was 18 percent in Portugal, 16 percent in Spain, and 14 percent in Ireland. (In the United States, the figure was only 5 percent, but US wind power has been expanding rapidly.) Moreover, in 2017 more than two hundred thousand wind turbines were in operation in more than eighty nations.

The World's First Wind-Powered House

Much of the ongoing revolution in global production of wind-generated power is attributable to the modern scientific understanding of wind and the typical patterns it forms above various regions of the continents. Also important have been steady technological advances in the equipment necessary to harness wind energy. These advances have allowed engineers to construct increasingly large and efficient wind turbines, for example.

Nevertheless, the idea of harnessing the wind to do work is far from new. In the ancient Middle East, for instance, people widely employed simple windmills in food production and other agricultural endeavors. In approximately 1000 CE, during the medieval era, those mechanical means of exploiting wind power spread into several European regions and kingdoms. The Netherlands was particularly receptive to these ideas and built thousands of windmills, many of which operated pumps. These allowed the locals to increase their arable (farmable) land by draining lakes and marshes.

During the 1800s science began to transform wind power into a source for creating electricity to power the swiftly expanding modern civilization. In 1887 Scottish researcher James Blyth built the first windmill that produced electricity. Standing 33 feet (10 m) high, the device featured cloth-covered wooden blades that

Wind turbines in Denmark (shown) were creating 21 percent of that country's electricity at the beginning of 2015, the highest percentage of any country. By 2017 more than two hundred thousand wind turbines were operating around the world.

harnessed the power of the wind. As they spun, they powered a primitive generator, which provided the electricity for the lamps in Blyth's modest cottage. That dwelling was the world's first house with wind-generated electrical power.

How Wind Turbines Work

This impressive feat was not lost on other scientists who saw the potential of wind power. Over time, various inventors and researchers introduced increasingly more advanced and efficient windmills, which came to be called wind turbines. Scientists also studied wind patterns in various locations in North

America and other continents. They found that certain areas—particularly open, fairly flat plains and the entrances to certain mountain passes—were noticeably windier than others. When possible, the experts decided, turbines should be erected on those sites to take advantage of their extraordinarily plentiful winds.

Wherever they are built, and no matter how large or complex they are, all modern wind turbines operate under the same basic principles. These devices feature propeller-like blades that move when they capture swathes of wind. Mounted on a tall and sturdy vertical shaft, the blades—which most often number two or three—are together called a rotor. A National Renewable Energy Laboratory (NREL) researcher explains the scientific concepts involved in a turbine's operation:

> A blade acts much like an airplane wing. When the wind blows, a pocket of low-pressure air forms on the downwind side of the blade. The low-pressure air pocket then pulls the blade toward it, causing the rotor to turn. This is called *lift*. The force of the lift is actually much stronger than the wind's force against the front side of the blade, which is called *drag*. The combination of lift and drag causes the rotor to spin like a propeller, and the turning shaft spins a generator to make electricity.[19]

Wind turbines can be used singly to power a specific house or other structure; farmers and ranchers in remote, windy areas sometimes install such devices to help reduce their electric bills or to pump water from wells. More and more often today wind turbines are employed in groups to produce larger amounts of energy to power grids that supply electricity to entire neighborhoods or towns.

Proper Siting

When multiple turbines are erected in clusters to power a grid, such a cluster has come to be called a wind farm (or wind power plant). At first glance it might seem that building a wind farm is a fairly straightforward proposition. That is, it seems that all a utility or other energy company has to do is acquire the necessary land and begin installing the turbines.

However, initiating such a project is far more complicated than that, according to the American Wind Energy Association (AWEA), the national trade organization for the US wind industry. The AWEA has collected extensive data about wind farms, including how they are funded and built. The ultimate success of such a farm, the AWEA explains, relies in large degree on choice of the proper site.

This process, called siting, begins with one or more individuals forming a company that will own and operate the wind farm. The company then must secure investors to fund the project, which can cost in the tens or even hundreds of millions of dollars or more. The company must also find a spot where there is enough wind to keep the turbines running. Plus, that land must be close enough to a major power grid to make daily electrical transmission from the farm to the grid practical. Next, the land must be purchased and any necessary government permits must be acquired. These and other issues need to be addressed, the AWEA says, "to move a wind project from development, through construction, and into operation. Failure to successfully navigate any one of these issues can result in a shelved project. On average, only one in ten projects originally conceived by a developer will actually get constructed and put into operation."[20]

A revealing example of this daunting process in action was the construction of the largest wind farm in the United States— the Alta Wind Energy Center (AWEA). It is located near Tehachapi Pass, about 75 miles (121 km) north of Los Angeles, California.

> **WORDS IN CONTEXT**
>
> **siting**
>
> The process of finding a site on which to build a wind farm.

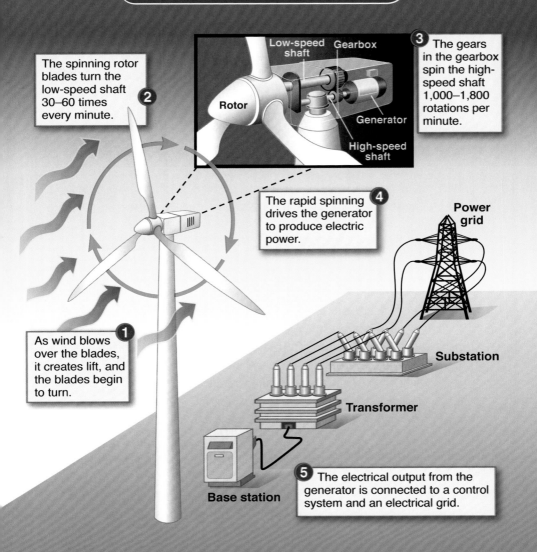

How Wind Turbines Work

The spinning rotor blades turn the low-speed shaft 30–60 times every minute. **2**

3 The gears in the gearbox spin the high-speed shaft 1,000–1,800 rotations per minute.

Low-speed shaft

Gearbox

Rotor

Generator

High-speed shaft

The rapid spinning drives the generator to produce electric power. **4**

Power grid

As wind blows over the blades, it creates lift, and the blades begin to turn. **1**

Substation

Transformer

5 The electrical output from the generator is connected to a control system and an electrical grid.

Base station

Source: US Department of Energy, "The Inside of a Wind Turbine." www.energy.gov.

According to the AWEA, it took the company that launched the project close to a decade to raise the $1.2 billion in funding, secure the land, and get the necessary government permits.

The company also found a utility—Southern California Edison—willing to buy and distribute the electricity the wind farm would eventually generate. Construction on the first of ten groups

CHOOSING WHERE TO BUILD WIND FARMS

Among the leading criteria that energy engineers and scientists look for when siting a wind farm's turbines are wind frequency and wind speeds in a potential site. The US Energy Information Administration here provides some details, including the physical setting of the Alta Wind Energy Center near California's Tehachapi Pass.

> Wind power plant owners must carefully plan where to position wind turbines and must consider how fast and how often the wind blows at the site. Wind speed typically increases with altitude and increases over open areas without windbreaks. Good sites for wind turbines include the tops of smooth, rounded hills; open plains and water; and mountain gaps that funnel and intensify wind. Wind speeds vary throughout the United States. Wind speeds also vary throughout the day and from season to season. In Tehachapi, California, the wind blows more frequently from April through October than it does in the winter. This fluctuation is a result of the extreme heat of the Mojave Desert during the summer months. As the hot air over the desert rises, the cooler, denser air above the Pacific Ocean rushes through the Tehachapi mountain pass to take its place. In a high altitude Great Plains state like Montana, strong winter winds channeled through the Rocky Mountain valleys create more intense winds during the winter.

US Energy Information Administration, "Renewable Wind." www.eia.gov.

of turbines began in 2010. Each group started producing electricity as soon as it was completed. When the last group is finished in 2019, the farm as a whole will create more than 1,500 MW (1.5 GW) of electricity per day, enough to power hundreds of thousands of homes.

Increasingly Large Arrays

The Alta Wind Energy Center is in several ways the natural offspring of earlier outsized arrays of wind turbines built in the United States. In fact, US energy companies and the scientists they hired pioneered the world's first large-scale wind farms. The original prototype was the Crotched Mountain Wind Farm in southern

New Hampshire. When it was built in 1980, wind power was still viewed by most Americans as a fringe idea; few thought it could realistically compete with coal and oil.

Not widely known at the time was that some scientists had long been working on the technology needed for wind farms. During the late 1970s they finally found a company willing to give that idea a try—US Windpower, formed by a group of recent graduates of the University of Massachusetts. The farm's twenty turbines, each of which generated only .3 MW of electricity, were quickly installed on the mountain. The onsite manager, Regina Wdowiak, proudly announced, "I definitely think this is the wave of the future. We are really caught in the infancy of this industry. No more is wind the funky energy that hippies are putting up."[21]

Although the Crotched Mountain farm went out of business a few years later, it had shown that using multiple wind turbines to help power a grid was both practical and promising. This encouraged others to take a chance, and several more wind-power companies formed between 1980 and 1984. One of these outfits, Fayette Manufacturing Corporation, constructed a huge wind farm in Altamont Pass in northern California. It opened in 1985 at partial capacity (because at that point only some of the turbines had been installed). When completed a while later, it featured 4,930 turbines, at the time making it the world's largest wind farm. Indeed, at that moment fully half of the world's wind energy was generated in Altamont Pass.

As arrays of turbines rapidly grew larger, many other huge wind farms, some of them in other countries, were soon constructed. Some, like the Alta and Altamont farms, were onshore, or erected on land. One of the biggest of the new onshore facilities is the Whitelee Wind Farm located about 9 miles (15 km) from Scotland's largest city, Glasgow. It began operation in 2008 and is now the United Kingdom's biggest wind farm, with 215 turbines that together create 539 MW of electricity daily.

Huge Offshore Facilities

During the same period in which the onshore Whitelee farm's turbines were installed, many of the other new wind farms were constructed offshore, in the relatively shallow waters on the continental coastlines. One prominent example among the several huge offshore wind farms built between 1995 and 2017 is the Thanet Wind Farm situated just off England's southeastern coast. The one hundred towering turbines in its array stand in water that varies in depth from 46 to 75 feet (14 to 23 m).

A row of wind turbines in the large Thanet Offshore Wind Farm stand in shallow waters off the coast of England. Keeping such offshore facilities stable on the sea floor is a daunting challenge for engineers.

While those turbines were under construction, the engineers had to deal with a daunting challenge faced by the builders of all the massive turbines employed in offshore wind farms. Namely, they had to successfully anchor and stabilize the turbines to ensure that water currents, waves, wind gusts, and storms would not topple them. "To stay steady," an expert observer explains, "turbines are anchored to the seafloor and to a narrow foundation dug 200 feet [61 m] underground. That anchoring, with help from very strong building materials with a corrosion-resistant coating, make the turbines stable enough to hold their own against wind and storms."[22]

By the time the Thanet facility opened in 2010, this standard anchoring process had been perfected. It was used with equal success and reliability soon afterward in the construction of the London Array, which began operation in 2013. The world's largest offshore wind farm, it is located in the outer estuary of the Thames River in southern England. The London Array features 175 enormous turbines, each standing 285 feet (87 m) tall. Each rotor is an astonishing 394 feet (120 m) across, or about the length of one and one-third football fields.

The Future of Wind Power

The use of wind power to create electricity is steadily increasing around the globe, and scientists and other experts regularly urge both governments and private investors to expand the industry still further. That will create more jobs, they point out. Also, wind energy is economical to produce, and investing in it boosts national economies. According to the AWEA, for instance, between 2007 and 2017 wind-power investments and production fed some $128 billion into the US economy.

Most important of all, the experts say, wind power is a clean alternative to using fossil fuels. "By expanding to 35 percent of the [US electrical] grid by 2050," an AWEA spokesperson states, "wind energy can cumulatively avoid more than 12.3 billion metric tons of carbon pollution."[23] That is roughly one-third of annual carbon emissions worldwide.

To help make this bright future for wind power possible, engineers and other scientists are constantly working on research and development projects to create new advances. Designing longer, lighter rotor blades is one example that has already paid off, and that trend is expected to continue. In addition, some scientists are looking into a seemingly radical notion: bladeless turbines. A Spanish company, appropriately named Vortex Bladeless, has already explored the idea of using a tall, thin tower that creates a spinning vortex, or whirlpool effect, in the surrounding air. Technology reporter Liz Stinson explains: "There are no gears, bolts, or mechanically moving parts, which they say makes the Vortex cheaper to manufacture and maintain. The founders claim their Vortex Mini, which stands at around 41 feet tall, can capture up to 40 percent of the wind's power during ideal conditions."[24]

> ## WORDS IN CONTEXT
>
> ### spinning vortex
> The whirlpool-like effect produced by experimental bladeless turbines.

Although there are few outwardly vocal critics of expanding wind power, some of them have called attention to some legitimate concerns. Perhaps the best known is the incidence of birds dying when they fly into wind turbines' spinning rotors. According to the many scientific studies so far conducted on this phenomenon, roughly two hundred thousand birds are killed this way each year in the United States.

A few scientists, notably at the NREL, have begun trying to find ways of avoiding these avian deaths. The most recent and promising one involves Houdini, a fifteen-year-old trained falcon. The NREL researchers asked Houdini's trainer to teach the bird to fly at the same height as average wind turbines while wearing a special tracking system provided by the NREL lab. That system allows the technicians in the lab to see Houdini as an image on a radar screen. The goal is to teach the technicians who operate the turbines in wind farms to better recognize radar images of large birds. That way, if one of those technicians sees images that appear to be birds moving toward a turbine, he or she can shut down the rotor until the birds are gone.

Whether or not science does manage to solve this problem, overall most experts on energy production agree that wind pow-

ARE BIRD DEATHS A NECESSARY
HAZARD OF HUMAN PROGRESS?

Some organizations that work with the wind power industry, including the NREL, are searching for ways to reduce the number of birds killed each year in collisions with wind turbines. The owners of various wind farms say they are open to suggestions for realistic ways to achieve this goal. However, the official position of the wind power industry as a whole is more pessimistic. Essentially, it holds that, although the loss of some two hundred thousand birds annually is unfortunate, for the time being it is impossible to avoid. Furthermore, it may need to be accepted as a necessary hazard of human progress. When questioned about the bird losses, the AWEA points out that they represent only a tiny fraction of the total avian fatalities caused by human civilization. To put the wind-power impacts on birds into perspective, the AWEA states, people must consider that "other causes of avian mortality are significantly greater." Those other causes, an AWEA spokesperson goes on, include

> collisions with buildings, which are estimated to kill 97 to 976 million birds annually; collisions with high-tension lines, which kill at least 130 million birds annually . . . cars, which may kill 80 million birds annually; [and] domestic cats, which historically have been estimated to kill hundreds of millions of songbirds and other bird species annually.

American Wind Energy Association, "Birds and Wind Energy." www.awea.org.

er's many positives outweigh its negatives. According to Windustry, an independent group that promotes future sustainable energy use,

In just a few short decades wind energy has matured dramatically, making wind one of the fastest growing sources of electricity in the world today. Due to technological advancements, policy initiatives, and economic drivers, wind energy is now able to make a cost-competitive contribution to our growing energy needs. [US] ingenuity and drive for independence are well suited to increased wind energy development in the future. Stay tuned to advancements at industry and policy levels as wind energy continues to grow.[25]

CHAPTER FOUR

Exploiting the Planet's Inexhaustible Heat

> **"The heat of the Earth is considered infinite; its use is only limited by technology and the associated costs, but the potential is there to provide enough energy to meet the power needs of humankind many times over."**
>
> —Geothermal Energy Association
>
> Geothermal Energy Association, "Potential Use." www.geo-energy.org.

One of the most impressive individual success stories of modern sustainable energy production can be found in the Mayacama Mountains, which are located about 72 miles (116 km) north of San Francisco, California. Called simply the Geysers, it is the world's largest geothermal field, with more than 350 geothermal wells that provide heat for the operation of twenty-two geothermal power plants. In turn, those facilities create about 60 percent of the electricity used in the four counties in the region stretching from just north of San Francisco northward to the Oregon border. Moreover, the geothermal energy from the Geysers field does more than make electricity. Like the energy mined from geothermal regions around the world, it is also used for the direct heating of homes and other buildings.

The plentiful supply of heat exploited by the Geysers and fields like it derives directly from geothermal energy—the heat energy contained beneath Earth's surface. Most of that heat is a by-product of the solar system's initial formation. Around 4.5 to

5 billion years ago the planets coalesced, or came together, from masses of gases and solid debris orbiting the infant Sun. These materials steadily contracted, becoming increasingly dense, and in doing so they grew extremely hot. As Earth's surface solidified, it trapped much of that heat in the planet's core. Very little of the core's heat has been lost over time. Indeed, even today the temperature at the planet's center is roughly 9,932°F (5,500°C).

Added to that astoundingly high heat generated by the planetary core, extra heat derives from radioactive elements beneath the ground. These unstable substances are in a constant state of decay, a process that generates a lot of heat. In addition, Earth's surface layer absorbs heat from the sunlight that relentlessly beats down on it.

The Geysers (shown), north of San Francisco, California, is the world's largest geothermal power facility. It taps 350 geothermal wells for heat used by twenty-two power plants to make electricity.

The combination of all these sources makes the planet's interior enormously hot. Scientists estimate that at any given moment some 42 million MW of heat energy exist in Earth's outer layers. One of the major advantages of that heat, the Geothermal Energy Association states, "is that it is constantly available. The constant flow of heat from the Earth ensures an inexhaustible and essentially limitless supply of energy for billions of years to come."[26]

Early Exploitation of Geothermal Energy

Geothermal is a modern word derived from the Greek roots *geo*, meaning "earth," and *thermos*, meaning "heat." Human use of geothermal heat is *not* strictly a modern phenomenon, however. For example, the ancient inhabitants of most of the continents were familiar with geysers, which are hot springs that sometimes shoot sprays or columns of steam and/or hot water into the air. The numerous hot springs contained in the famous Geysers field in northern California were well known to the Native Americans who lived in that area, including the Pomo, Miwaok, and Wappo peoples. These individuals used the inviting warm springs for heating, cooking, and bathing. Settlers discovered the Geysers field during the mid-1800s and soon erected spas and hotels in the area. One of those facilities, the Geysers Resort Hotel, regularly attracted well-to-do celebrities, among them presidents Ulysses S. Grant and Theodore Roosevelt and humorist Mark Twain.

In Asia and Europe, meanwhile, hot springs were also exploited for millennia. As early as the 200s BCE, Chinese rulers erected a palace beside the Huaqing hot springs at the foot of Mt. Li and used them for heating and bathing. During the same period the residents of the Roman town of Pompeii built their own bathing facilities atop hot springs heated by the nearby active volcano Mt. Vesuvius. Hot springs in England and Iceland were used similarly in both ancient and medieval times.

Later, modern science and industry came to see the potential of such thermal sites. The first modern industrial use of geothermal hot springs began in 1827 in Larderello, Italy. Italian scientists found a way to employ steam rising from a hot spring there to mine boric acid from volcanic mud. In 1892 the town of Boise,

Idaho, installed the first geothermal district heating system, which pumped water from a local hot spring to a few homes and businesses. The first case of geothermal electricity production occurred in a geothermal plant constructed in Larderello in 1911. It remained the only creator of geothermal electricity until New Zealand built a similar facility in 1958.

US GEOTHERMAL ENERGY PRODUCTION

Today the United States is a major leader in modern geothermal energy production. But it took more than a century for the country to acquire that status. The first serious US use of geothermal energy began in 1892 when engineers in Boise, Idaho, began piping hot water from a nearby spring into the town to heat a few homes and other buildings. In 1900, inspired by Boise's example, the town of Klamath Falls, Oregon, began the same practice. The first time that a commercial building in the United States was heated solely by a ground source heat pump was in 1948 in Portland, Oregon. The country's first major geothermal power plant opened in 1960 in the Geysers field in northern California. In 1981 US scientists first started testing the binary method of powering a geothermal station. Geothermal power production started in the massive Puna hot springs field in Hawaii in 1992.

More and more geothermal power plants opened in the years that followed, and by 2017 the country had sixty-nine such facilities, generating more than 3.4 GW of electricity annually. In pure energy generation, that is equivalent to burning some 25 million barrels of oil per year or 6 million tons (5.3 million metric t) of coal annually. International energy agencies estimate that during the period of 2015 through 2017 the United States created about 30 percent of all the geothermal-generated electricity in the world.

Modern Geothermal Heating

Boise still heats many of its homes and businesses using geothermal energy, and it is not alone. In 2017 more than seventy countries used direct geothermal heating, especially in areas where underground hot springs are located near or on Earth's surface. In addition to the United States, those nations include Japan, Indonesia, New Zealand, Turkey, Iceland, the Philippines, Kenya, and Italy. One thing all these countries have in common is that they contain multiple regions where volcanic and other subterranean heat sources come to or close to the surface.

The water that flows underground in those areas is hot enough that it can provide direct heating of human homes and other structures. Municipal- and state-run geothermal utilities in such regions take advantage of that fact by tapping directly into the hot springs. Boise's main geothermal system is an often-copied example. The Boise Public Works Department pumps hot water at temperatures in excess of 170°F (77°C) from a hot spring located in the hills outside of the town. Flowing into metal radiators, this water heats large numbers of buildings in downtown Boise and the nearby Boise State University campus. In 2015 the system ranked as the biggest single example of direct geothermal heating in the United States. "Our geothermal system is a clean and affordable source of energy," Boise's mayor, David Bieter, states. "Boise is fortunate to have this natural asset; it's our duty to maximize its effectiveness by extending its reach as far as possible."[27]

Direct piping from a hot spring is not the only method of obtaining hot water for geothermal heating systems. Some towns in the United States and other countries have no surface hot springs nearby, although they are located in areas of high geothermal activity. Instead, they drill wells in order to reach deeper pockets of hot water and/or steam.

Tapping the Ground's Surface Layers

Another way that geothermal energy is used for direct heating of buildings does not rely on underground water in isolated spots. Instead, it takes advantage of the fact that the ground everywhere, from the surface down to a depth of about 20 feet (6 m), contains heat. Moving deeper into the next layer, which measures a couple thousand feet in thickness, the ground contains even more heat. That heat can be tapped to heat a home in the winter months. The heat thus obtained from geothermal energy can also be removed from the house to cool the structure in the warmer months.

The chief means of siphoning heat from the ground's surface layers uses a device that English scientists introduced during the 1850s, American scientists perfected in 1948, and Swedish scientists further advanced in 1979. It is called a ground source heat pump (sometimes inaccurately referred to as a geothermal heat pump). It has three main parts: the exchanger, which either pulls

> **WORDS IN CONTEXT**
>
> **exchanger**
>
> In a ground source heat pump, a device that either pulls heat out of the ground or puts it back in.

heat out of the ground or puts it back in; a pump unit that delivers or removes the heat from the house's interior; and a series of ducts that carry warm or cool air through the structure.

The heat exchanger consists of a group of thin coiled pipes called a loop, which the installer buries in the shallow ground near the house. A fluid, most often a mixture of water and antifreeze, passes through the pipes. In the process, the water steadily absorbs heat from the surrounding ground and passes it on to the pump. According to the National Renewable Energy Laboratory (NREL), pumps of this kind

> work much like refrigerators, which make a cool place (the inside of the refrigerator) cooler by transferring heat to a relatively warm place (the surrounding room), making it warmer. In the winter, the heat pump removes heat from the heat exchanger and pumps it into the indoor air delivery system, moving heat from the ground to the building's interior. In the summer, the process is reversed, and the heat pump moves heat from the indoor air into the heat exchanger, effectively moving the heat from indoors to the ground. The heat removed from the indoor air during the summer can also be used to heat water, providing a free source of hot water.[28]

Even after the Swedish version of the ground source heat pump appeared during the late 1970s, these devices continued to be used mainly in houses and other relatively small buildings. Versions that could provide heating and cooling of a skyscraper did not yet exist. Advances during the 1990s finally allowed this to happen. In 1998 the Foundation House in New York City became the first large-scale structure to get all of its heating and cooling from geothermal energy. The exchangers of its heat pumps were installed in holes drilled some 1,500 feet (456 m) into the Manhattan bedrock. "We're not going to change the world with one little building," the structure's owner, Theodore W. Kheel, told the press. "But we can set an example. Geothermal will be our best expression of what can be accomplished. It's beneficial for the environment and will save tremendously on electricity."[29]

Geothermal Electricity Production

Scientists continue to make technical advances in heat pumps that transfer geothermal heat directly into human-made structures. Some of those same researchers, including scientists at the NREL, have also been making periodic strides in the technology of geothermal power production. That is the geothermal industry's preferred name for the generation of electricity using geothermal energy.

Two years after the world's second geothermal power plant opened in New Zealand in 1958, a US company built the first American version in the Geysers geothermal field. By 2017 the number of nations with electricity-generating geothermal plants had risen to twenty-four. Their total output of electrical power was then around 13 GW. Depending on the size of those countries' populations and electricity demands, some generate a fair proportion of their electricity via geothermal sources. Kenya, El Salvador, the Philippines, and Iceland all make more than 15 percent of their electricity from geothermal energy. In part because the United States has a much larger electrical demand and still uses a lot of fossil fuels to make electricity, in 2017 only about .4 percent of US electricity came from geothermal sources. But that proportion is expected to rise considerably as new, more advanced geothermal technologies are introduced in the near future.

Geothermal power plants employ three methods of creating electricity. The oldest and simplest is the dry steam process, which taps into steam created in geothermal hot springs near Earth's surface. A dry steam plant is erected beside or atop the hot spring, and the steam rises directly into one or more turbines. As they spin, they power an electrical generator. The geothermal plants in the Geysers field use the dry steam method.

One of Iceland's many active volcanoes is shown from the air. Volcanic activity has provided geothermal power to Iceland and many other volcanically active countries for centuries.

The second and most commonly employed geothermal method of making electricity is the flash steam process. It requires drilling wells to find deeper underground pockets of water at temperatures in excess of 360°F (182°C). The hot water flows up through a well until it enters a so-called flash tank, where the pressure is much less than it is where the water came from. The lower pressure causes the water to boil into steam, which runs the plant's turbines. Any excess hot water is sent back into the ground. The Hellisheidi Station in western Iceland (the third-largest geothermal plant in the world) is one of the many geothermal power plants that employ the flash steam method.

The third method of making electricity at geothermal power plants—called binary steam—is widely viewed as the wave of the future. Scientists are still perfecting this method, and each new binary steam plant that opens is technologically more advanced than those preceding it. Such a facility employs steam produced by a different liquid than water. Hot water is used only to heat that secondary liquid. As a member of the Union of Concerned Scientists explains, in a binary plant "the hot water is passed through a heat exchanger, where it heats a second liquid—such as isobutane—in a closed loop. Isobutane boils at a lower temperature than water, so it is more easily converted into steam to run the turbine."[30] The term *closed loop* refers to the fact that the isobutane and water never come into contact with each other, so each remains pristine and totally reusable.

The Te Huka Geothermal Power Station, which opened in 2010 near Taupo, New Zealand, is a binary geothermal plant. So are the three plants in the Mammoth Geothermal Complex in California. In these cutting-edge geothermal facilities, no pollution of any kind is emitted into the environment. Also, their systems neatly recycle the materials used. For example, once the hot water heats up the isobutane, that water is pumped back into the ground at a depth where it reheats and becomes available for the next cycle of power production.

Future Advances in Geothermal Power

Finding ways to make binary geothermal plants more efficient is only one of many ways that scientists are making strides in geothermal energy production. Another promising area of research and development is the area of engineered reservoirs, also known as an enhanced geothermal system (EGS). These are deep underground chambers that scientists and engineers carve out of solid rock using advanced drilling techniques.

The rock at that depth is very hot. But in most such reservoirs there are few or no paths for subterranean water streams to pass though on their way to a power plant. Scientists are trying to find ways of remedying that situation, which would allow for considerable expansion of geothermal power plants around the globe. As the US Office of Energy Efficiency and Renewable Energy states, "During EGS development, underground fluid pathways are safely created and their size and connectivity increased. These enhanced pathways allow fluid to circulate throughout the hot rock and carry heat to the surface to generate electricity."[31]

GEOTHERMAL ENERGY FROM WASTEWATER

One of the many areas of geothermal energy production in which scientists are making steady advances is finding ways for geothermal plants to use wastewater left over from oil and natural gas drilling. An online article by the Union of Concerned Scientists explains the process:

An MIT [Massachusetts Institute of Technology] study estimated that the United States has the potential to develop 44,000 MWs of geothermal capacity by 2050 by coproducing geothermal electricity at oil and gas fields—primarily in the Southeast and southern Plains states. The study projected that such advanced geothermal systems could supply 10 percent of U.S. base-load electricity by 2050, given R&D [research and development] and deployment over the next 10 years. According to DOE [the US Department of Energy], an average of 25 billion barrels of hot water is produced in United States oil and gas wells each year. This water, which has historically been viewed as an inconvenience to well operators, could be harnessed to produce up to 3 gigawatts of clean, reliable base-load energy. This energy could not only reduce greenhouse gas emissions, it could also increase profitability and extend the economic life of existing oil and gas field infrastructure. The DOE's Geothermal Technologies Office is working toward a goal of achieving widespread production of low-temperature geothermal power by 2020.

Union of Concerned Scientists, "How Geothermal Energy Works." www.ucsusa.org.

Another area of cutting-edge geothermal research involves finding new mapping methods that will allow scientists to more easily locate underground hot spots. Although, in general, the deeper humans drill the hotter the rocks get, some areas are hotter than others. Those hotter underground pockets are the regions that are the prime targets of the geothermal energy industry.

Scientists are also hoping to better exploit a material known as geothermal brine. Put simply, it is hot water from deep underground that is heavily mixed with various minerals. These minerals are potentially very valuable to a wide range of industries. Researchers are trying to find ways to extract deeply seated brine and to separate out the minerals. That way the hot water could be used to run geothermal power plants and the minerals could be sold for a profit to companies around the world.

The steady appearance of cutting-edge technology in geothermal heating and electrical production suggests that the future of this energy industry is bright. "These exciting new developments in geothermal will be supported by unprecedented levels of federal R&D [research and development] funding," the Union of Concerned Scientists points out. Such investments "are already beginning to expand the horizons of geothermal energy production and will likely continue to produce significant net benefits in the future."[32]

CHAPTER FIVE

Hydrogen's Potentially Limitless Power

"Hydrogen as a fuel source for energy, whether used to produce electricity via a hydrogen fuel cell or used as a primary fuel to drive generators and automobile engines, has many positive advantages, balanced with very few negative consequences or drawbacks."

—Alternative Energy, a website dedicated to educating people about renewable forms of energy

Alternative Energy, "Hydrogen Fuel Cells—Hydrogen Power." www.altenergy.org.

In 2016 the Consumer Electronics Show held its annual meeting in Las Vegas, Nevada. One of the most intriguing of the many cutting-edge devices on display was presented by the British high-tech company Intelligent Energy. It was the prototype, or test model, for a hydrogen-powered smartphone that can be used for an entire day on a single charge. Its hydrogen fuel creates virtually zero pollution and poses no danger of catching fire, as the lithium batteries of many recently sold electronic devices do. The only drawback of Intelligent Energy's futuristic smartphone is that it is still very expensive to recharge. But the company points out that it is working diligently on ways to get that cost down during the next few years.

The power source behind that phone, along with high-tech cars and all sorts of other emerging devices and energy systems, is hydrogen, the simplest and most abundant element in the universe. Used in devices called fuel cells, as well as in other ways, it is powerful, versatile, clean burning, safe, can be stored for later use, and can be easily piped or otherwise conveyed to where it is needed. In addition, because hydrogen atoms are so abundant in the universe, supplies of it are, for all intents and purposes, limitless. That makes it a potent source of sustainable energy.

Scientists who are hard at work developing hydrogen power envision a future in which national economies are driven in large part by hydrogen energy sources. In 2016, they point out, the global hydrogen market was already worth more than $100 billion, and that figure is estimated to grow to at least $152 billion by 2021. Also, they say, in the coming decades hydrogen power can potentially greatly reduce civilization's present dependence on fossil fuels and thereby contribute to a cleaner environment.

Where Is Hydrogen Located?

In order to use hydrogen for electricity and other types of power, scientists must first locate supplies of that element. Fortunately, finding hydrogen is easy because it exists virtually everywhere, although it takes numerous forms. The simplest form of hydrogen is hydrogen gas. It exists in enormous quantities in the Sun and other stars. Obtaining supplies of hydrogen gas from stars is not yet possible—and might never be possible. Nor can scientists get significant amounts of the gas on Earth's surface. Because hydrogen is the lightest of all the elements, in gaseous form it is even lighter than air. As a result, the small amounts that occur on the surface rise up into the atmosphere and disappear into space.

The planet still has plenty of hydrogen, however. It is locked up in thousands upon thousands of compounds in which hydrogen is bound together with one or more other elements. The most familiar of these is water. A molecule of water is composed of two hydrogen atoms and one oxygen atom. Hydrogen is also found in numerous substances inside and atop Earth's crust. Among them are oil, gasoline, and other petroleum products; nearly all plants; dairy products; and many kinds of alcohols and acids. There are also plentiful amounts of hydrogen in methane gas, of which untold billions of tons exist on Earth. Methane is in rice fields, garbage dumps, the waste products of all animals,

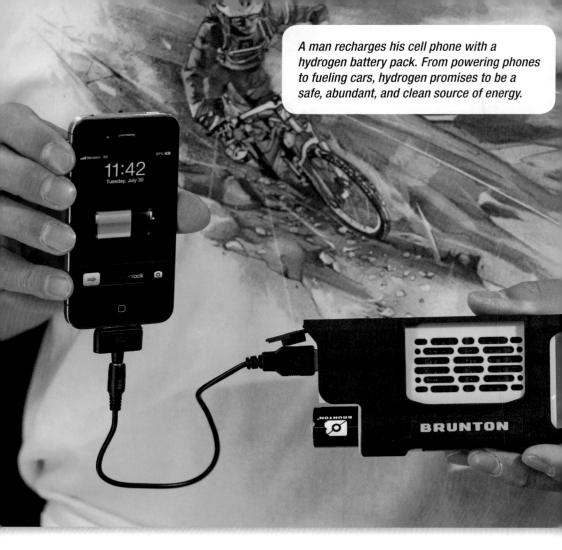

A man recharges his cell phone with a hydrogen battery pack. From powering phones to fueling cars, hydrogen promises to be a safe, abundant, and clean source of energy.

and termite nests, to name only a few of its sources. A helpful online sustainable energy information source lists some others:

> Methane is the main component of natural gas. So leakage throughout this industry releases methane straight into the atmosphere. [Coal] is another important source of methane emissions. In coal formation, pockets of methane get trapped around and within the rock. Coal mining related activities (extraction, crushing, distribution, etc.) release some of this trapped methane. [Also, microbes living in] wetlands are the largest natural source of methane. This produces 78 percent of natural methane emissions.[33]

Producing Hydrogen for Energy Use

Clearly, therefore, an immense quantity of hydrogen exists on Earth, and only a tiny percentage of it could, in theory, power human civilization for many thousands of years. However, because nearly all of the available hydrogen is locked up in compounds with other elements, scientists must first separate it from those compounds before it can be used for energy generation. Of the two most common techniques presently employed for producing such supplies of usable hydrogen, one is called steam reforming.

It uses intense blasts of scalding steam to separate the hydrogen atoms from the carbon atoms in methane. Although the process is quite cost effective, it has a serious drawback: it leaks gaseous by-products that contribute to the atmospheric warming associated with climate change.

Intent on avoiding this problem, some scientists are increasingly turning to the other principal method of producing usable hydrogen. Known as electrolysis, it is a process that separates the hydrogen from the oxygen in water. It works by passing an electric current through a container of water having a positively charged terminal, or anode, on one end and a negatively charged terminal, or cathode, on the other. The bolt of electricity momentarily weakens the strong bonds that hold the atoms together. When that occurs, masses of hydrogen atoms collect at the cathode, and smaller numbers of oxygen atoms crowd around the anode.

> **WORDS IN CONTEXT**
>
> **steam reforming**
> The process of using scalding hot water to separate the hydrogen and oxygen atoms that make up water.

Electrolysis is a very efficient way of producing pure hydrogen. It, too, has a drawback, however, namely that for the time being it is very expensive. That means it is not cost effective for obtaining the large amounts of hydrogen that would be required to run a power plant capable of making electricity for the grid.

Hoping to meet this requirement, various scientific labs, including some at the National Renewable Energy Laboratory (NREL) and in private companies, are experimenting with new ways to create pure hydrogen. One method is the so-called Hazer process, conceived in labs at the University of Western Australia. This approach uses methane-rich natural gas, which contains large amounts of hydrogen and carbon. In a chemical process conducted in a lab, the hydrogen and carbon within the methane separate out, thereby freeing the hydrogen for energy production or other uses.

One highly desirable aspect of the technique is that it does more than just free lots of usable hydrogen. In addition, the separated carbon can be captured as pure graphite, a mineral used by hundreds of industries. "This graphite is a saleable product, giving the

The world's livestock, especially cattle, is a major source of the methane gas released into the Earth's atmosphere every day. Methane could be used as a source of hydrogen for fuel cells.

process two valuable products rather than just one and thereby reduces the cost of the process," explains Geoff Pocock of the Hazer Group, which is helping to promote the process. "And with would-be carbon emissions instead captured in the form of solid graphite, Hazer can produce [large quantities of] 'clean' hydrogen."[34]

Hydrogen Fuel Cells

In whatever manner scientists produce usable quantities of hydrogen, their primary goal is to put it to work in the creation of energy, particularly in the form of electricity. In recent years the most common approach to achieving this goal has been perfecting hydrogen fuel cells. A fuel cell is a device that directly converts the chemical energy in hydrogen into electricity. The US Office of Energy Efficiency and Renewable Energy explains a fuel cell's basic workings, saying,

> Fuel cells work like batteries, but they do not run down or need recharging. They produce electricity and heat as long as fuel is supplied. A fuel cell consists of two electrodes—a negative electrode (or anode) and a positive electrode (or cathode)—sandwiched around an electrolyte [a gel that conducts electricity]. Hydrogen is fed to the anode, and air [containing oxygen] is fed to the cathode [and the result is] a flow of electricity.[35]

Among the impressive advantages of fuel cells is that the only by-products they create are pure water and heat. This means that they are pollution free. In addition, fuel cells cannot explode, burn, or otherwise do damage, so they are safe to handle and use.

A single fuel cell generates a fairly small amount of electrical current. So scientists and engineers usually combine several of them, a practice called stacking. The potential applications of these stacks are many and varied. A

HOW A HYDROGEN POWER PLANT WILL WORK

In 2017 no hydrogen power plants designed to generate electricity had yet been built. However, scientists continue to work hard on designs that will make the necessary technologies cost effective in the near future. One problem they face is that it remains fairly expensive to produce enough hydrogen to fuel the plant in the first place. Once that difficulty has been satisfactorily overcome, the hydrogen will be used in a proposed plant in the form of fuel cells. Tens of thousands of them will create a large flow of electricity. Some of that energy will be dispensed to a local grid to power nearby homes and businesses. Any excess electricity produced will be stored in special batteries on the plant's grounds.

In 2006 a hydrogen power plant was scheduled to be built over the course of a few years in Peterhead, Scotland. That site was chosen because it lies near the Sleipner natural gas field in the North Sea. The field's huge supplies of natural gas seemed to guarantee large amounts of hydrogen that would not have to be shipped at higher cost from more distant sources. After a number of delays, however, the Peterhead plant was canceled in 2011 in large part due to the enormous costs involved in constructing such a futuristic prototype facility.

few small fuel cells can power a laptop computer or a cell phone, for example. A stack of larger fuel cells is capable of providing backup electricity for a building or bringing electrical power to a house in a remote region that is not connected to the power grid. In fact, hydrogen fuel cells can be used to do most of the jobs that conventional batteries do.

Hydrogen Fuel Cell Vehicles

One of the chief uses of conventional batteries is to help power cars, trucks, buses, boats, and other motor vehicles. So a major focus of present cutting-edge research on fuel cells is related to powering such machines. Indeed, scientists hope that in the decades to come hydrogen fuel cells will largely replace the fossil fuels that now run most cars and trucks. As the Union of Concerned Scientists puts it,

Unlike conventional vehicles, which run on gasoline or diesel, fuel cell cars and trucks combine hydrogen and oxygen to produce electricity, which runs a motor. Since they're powered entirely by electricity, fuel cell vehicles are considered electric vehicles ("EVs")—but unlike other EVs, their range and refueling processes are comparable to conventional cars and trucks. Converting hydrogen gas into electricity produces only water and heat as a byproduct, meaning fuel cell vehicles don't create tailpipe pollution when they're driven.[36]

A number of automobile companies have already built prototypes of cars that run on fuel cells. One is BMW's Gran Turismo fuel-cell prototype. In road tests conducted in 2015, the car traveled 310 miles (500 km) without needing refueling. One witness to the test commented that "the Gran Turismo handled like any other electric car, except for a hissing sound during sharp acceleration

Many automobile companies have produced concept cars that run on hydrogen fuel cells. Pictured is the hydrogen fuel system of a Toyota model.

Hydrogen tank

from a pump passing hydrogen and air through the fuel cells."[37] By 2017 several other fuel-cell car prototypes had been introduced, among them the Honda Clarity, Audi Q5-FCEV, Toyota Mirai, and Hyundai Tucson FCEV.

Although the potential for such hydrogen-powered vehicles is promising, two factors still keep them from being mass-produced. First, as prototypes employing cutting-edge technology, they are very expensive to make. Second, refueling these vehicles requires either specialized fuel-cell stations (of which very few have been built) or conventional gas stations that carry fuel-cell refueling equipment. The vast majority do not yet do so. Partly for these reasons, the auto market remains dominated by cheaper conventional vehicles that run on fossil fuels.

Hydrogen Energy's Bright Future

Some scientists presently working on hydrogen-based energy systems are attempting to create still more efficient fuel cells. Others are concentrating their efforts on finding effective, inexpensive ways to bring hydrogen not only to future refueling stations but also to homes, businesses, factories, skyscrapers, and other places that want to exploit its energy. The specialized pipes and other means of shipping the hydrogen are already being called the hydrogen energy infrastructure.

In that future system, scientists say, hydrogen gas will likely be produced in a few key places using a more advanced type of electrolysis than now available. Next, workers at the production plant will compress the gas so that it can be inserted in the transmission pipeline. The latter will carry the hydrogen to dispensing terminals in various cities and towns. From there, the gas can be used in fuel cells assembled on the spot or else stored for future use.

Even more cutting edge is present research into the most futuristic and most powerful hydrogen-based technology. Called

> **WORDS IN CONTEXT**
>
> **hydrogen fusion**
> Also called nuclear fusion, the process of forcefully driving two hydrogen atoms together to generate energy.

hydrogen fusion, or nuclear fusion, it is also potentially the most powerful of all sources of renewable energy. In the words of science writer Nathaniel Scharping,

> Nuclear fusion has long been considered the "holy grail" of energy research. It represents a nearly limitless source of energy that is clean, safe and self-sustaining. Ever since its existence was first theorized in the 1920s by English physicist Arthur Eddington, nuclear fusion has captured the imaginations of scientists and science-fiction writers alike.[38]

NUCLEAR FUSION SIMPLIFIED

Most people are unfamiliar with the concept and terminology surrounding hydrogen fusion, also called nuclear fusion. Science writer Cathal O'Connell provides this helpful, simplified explanation of what hydrogen fusion is, ongoing attempts to create fusion in labs, and why conducting such research is so difficult.

Atoms are the really small bits from which we are all made. Inside each atom, when you strip away the shells of electrons, is an even smaller bit at the core—the nucleus. It turns out that when you join two small nuclei to make a bigger one, an enormous amount of energy is released—about 10 million times more energy than the puny chemical reactions that power most of our technology, such as burning oil, coal, or the gasoline in your car. We know fusion works because it goes on in the core of the sun. [It] takes a lot of energy to get [fusion] going and typically that means a temperature of millions of degrees. This is because atomic nuclei have a love-hate relationship. Each nucleus has a strong positive charge so they repel one another. To kick-start fusion, you have to overcome this repulsive barrier by ramming two nuclei together incredibly hard. That's what happens in the core of the sun. [Hundreds] of research scale reactors have been built around the world. They are usually engineering marvels designed to contain hydrogen nuclei at 100 million degrees C [212 million°F], or implode a nuclear pellet using massive lasers.

Cathal O'Connell, "Getting Primed for Fusion Power," *Cosmos*, April 26, 2016. https://cosmosmagazine.com.

Hydrogen fusion also works in a way that, in its basics, is fairly easy to understand. In theory, a scientist takes two hydrogen atoms and forces them together with enormous force. This causes them to fuse (hence the term *fusion*), which creates a chemical/physical reaction that releases a burst of energy as a by-product. Now imagine countless trillions of hydrogen atoms fusing all at once, as happens in the Sun's deep interior. Indeed, the tremendous outpouring of energy thus produced is what makes the Sun and other stars shine.

For producing electricity for humanity, hydrogen fusion is very different from nuclear fission, in which atoms split to produce energy. Whereas present nuclear plants use fission, future ones will employ fusion to produce a great deal more power. Also, fusion plants will produce no significant radioactivity or other dangerous pollutants.

Scientists in the United States, Russia, and several other nations have been conducting intensive research into Earth-based fusion power for more than three decades. The problem so far has been that an immense amount of heat—in the range of tens of millions of degrees—is required to make fusion happen. The one-of-a-kind equipment required to create so much heat is fantastically expensive at present.

Yet there *have* been glimmers of hope. In 2014 scientists at the Lawrence Livermore National Laboratory in California used lasers to compress a tiny mass of hydrogen and produced a small-scale fusion reaction lasting a fraction of a second. Similar initial successes occurred between 2014 and 2017 in labs in Germany, France, and China. "Cracking fusion power would be one of the great technological achievements of the 21st century," says science writer Cathal O'Connell, "providing almost limitless power with few drawbacks."[39] Today, scientists are confident that fusion power will eventually become part of a package containing solar, wind, geothermal, and other forms of renewable energy. There is virtually no disagreement in the scientific community that that package promises to cleanly and reliably power human civilization for thousands of years to come.

SOURCE NOTES

Introduction: Renewable Energy to Run People's Homes

1. Quoted in David Glickson, "NREL Innovates Today for the Homes of Tomorrow," National Renewable Energy Laboratory, June 15, 2015. www.nrel.gov.
2. Glickson, "NREL Innovates Today for the Homes of Tomorrow."
3. Quoted in Glickson, "NREL Innovates Today for the Homes of Tomorrow."

Chapter One: A World Filled with Renewables

4. US Office of Energy Efficiency and Renewable Energy, "Renewable Energy Technology Basics," US Department of Energy. https://energy.gov.
5. Quoted in Bill Kovarik, "The Surprising History of Sustainable Energy," *Source* (blog), March 29, 2011. https://sustainable history.wordpress.com.
6. Werner von Siemens, "On the Electromotive Action of Illuminated Selenium, Discovered by Mr. Fitts of New York," *Van Nostrand's Engineering Magazine,* vol. 32, 1885, pp. 514–16.
7. Brazilian Sugarcane Industry Association, "Ethanol." http://sugarcane.org.
8. Union of Concerned Scientists, "Benefits of Renewable Energy Use." www.ucsusa.org.

Chapter Two: Harnessing Sunlight's Vast Energies

9. Robert Barnstone, "Solar on Ice," *Texas Monthly,* October 1977, p. 152.
10. International Energy Agency, "Solar Energy Perspectives: Executive Summary," 2011. www.iea.org.
11. Quoted in Wolfgang Palz, *Power for the World: The Emergence of Electricity from the Sun.* Singapore: Pan Stanford, 2010, p. 6.
12. Quoted in Palz, *Power for the World,* p. 9.

13. Katie Fehrenbacher, "How the Rise of a Mega-Panel Solar Farm Shows Us the Future of Energy," Gigaom, January 25, 2015. https://gigaom.com.
14. National Renewable Energy Laboratory, "Concentrating Solar Power Basics." www.nrel.gov.
15. National Renewable Energy Laboratory, "Solar Water Heating." www.nrel.gov.
16. US Department of Energy, "Passive Solar Home Design." https://energy.gov.
17. US Department of Energy, "Passive Solar Home Design."
18. International Energy Agency, "Solar Energy Perspectives."

Chapter Three: Clean, Inexpensive Wind Power

19. National Renewable Energy Laboratory, "Wind Energy Basics." www.nrel.gov.
20. American Wind Energy Association, "Wind Energy Is Beneficial to Wildlife; Industry Proactively Addresses Impacts." www.awea.org.
21. Quoted in Abby Kessler, "Gone with the Wind: When Crotched Mountain Had a Wind Farm," *Monadnock Ledger-Transcript,* February 9, 2017. www.ledgertranscript.com.
22. Brendan Cole, "The US Is Finally Getting Its First Offshore Wind Farm," *Wired,* July 28, 2016. www.wired.com.
23. American Wind Energy Association, "The Truth About Wind Power," *Into the Wind* (blog). www.aweablog.org.
24. Liz Stinson, "The Future of Wind Turbines: No Blades," *Wired,* May 15, 2015. www.wired.com.
25. Windustry, "History and Future of Wind Energy." www.windustry.org.

Chapter Four: Exploiting the Planet's Inexhaustible Heat

26. Geothermal Energy Association, "Basics." http://geo-energy.org.
27. Quoted in Mike Crapo, "Geothermal Expanding Across Broadway Bridge," July 7, 2010. www.crapo.senate.gov.
28. National Renewable Energy Laboratory, "Geothermal Heat Pump Basics." www.nrel.gov.

29. Quoted in Andrew C. Revkin, "New Building Will Use a Geo-thermal Energy System," *New York Times,* April 20, 1997. www.nytimes.com.

30. Union of Concerned Scientists, "How Geothermal Energy Works." www.ucsusa.org.

31. US Office of Energy Efficiency and Renewable Energy, "Energy Department Announces $18 Million for Innovative Projects to Advance Geothermal Energy," US Department of Energy. https://energy.gov.

32. Union of Concerned Scientists, "How Geothermal Energy Works."

Chapter Five: Hydrogen's Potentially Limitless Power

33. What's Your Impact?, "Main Sources of Methane Emissions." http://whatsyourimpact.org.

34. Quoted in Mychealla Rice, "Producing Clean Hydrogen with Near-Zero Carbon Emissions Using the Hazer Process," *AZo-Cleantech,* September 16, 2016. www.azocleantech.com.

35. US Office of Energy Efficiency and Renewable Energy, "Fuel Cell Basics," US Department of Energy. https://energy.gov.

36. Union of Concerned Scientists, "How Do Hydrogen Fuel Cell Vehicles Work?" www.ucsusa.org.

37. Elizabeth Behrmann, "BMW Pushes Fuel-Cell Car Development with First Street Tests," *Bloomberg News*, July 1, 2015. www.bloomberg.com.

38. Nathaniel Scharping, "Why Nuclear Fusion Is Always 30 Years Away." *Crux* (blog), *Discover,* March 23, 2016. http://blogs.discovermagazine.com.

39. Cathal O'Connell, "Getting Primed for Fusion Power," *Cosmos,* April 26, 2016. https://cosmosmagazine.com.

FIND OUT MORE

Books

Sam B. Badger, *Alternative Energy.* Charleston, SC: Amazon Digital Services, 2016.

Kenneth E. Barnes, *Solar Electric: How Does It Work?* Charleston, SC: Amazon Digital Services, 2016.

Anne Cunningham, *Critical Perspectives on Fossil Fuels vs. Renewable Energy.* Berkeley Heights, NJ: Enslow, 2017.

Robert Green, *How Renewable Energy Is Changing Society.* San Diego: ReferencePoint Press, 2015.

James Powell and Jesse Powell, *Silent Earth: Will Humans Give Up Fossil Fuels?* Charleston, SC: Amazon Digital Services, 2016.

Websites

National Renewable Energy Laboratory, "Geothermal Electricity Production Basics" (www.nrel.gov/workingwithus/re-geo-elec-production.html). This helpful site presents information on the existing methods of producing electricity in geothermal plants and provides links to subsites about facilities, ongoing research, energy education, and more.

US Office of Energy Efficiency and Renewable Energy, "Fuel Cells" (https://energy.gov/eere/fuelcells/fuel-cells). Here, a branch of the US Department of Energy presents a clear picture of what fuel cells are and how they work, along with plenty of links to articles on hydrogen production, hydrogen storage, the uses of hydrogen in manufacturing, and more.

US Office of Energy Efficiency and Renewable Energy, "How Do Wind Turbines Work?" (https://energy.gov/eere/wind/how-do-wind-turbines-work). This site provides helpful diagrams showing how wind turbines work as well as numerous links to articles on the history of turbines, research and development, wind farms, and much more.

Internet Sources

Katie Fehrenbacher, "How the Rise of a Mega-Panel Solar Farm Shows Us the Future of Energy," Gigaom, January 20, 2015. https://gigaom.com/2015/01/20/a-special-report-the-rise-of-a-mega-solar-panel-farm-why-its-important.

Andrew Follett, "Scientists Think This Simple Software Fix Could Make Nuclear Fusion a Reality," *Daily Caller,* February 13, 2017. http://dailycaller.com/2017/02/13/scientists-think-this-simple-software-fix-could-make-nuclear-fusion-a-reality.

Brian Merchant, "In the Future, Will Wind Turbines Be Everywhere?," HowStuffWorks Science. http://science.howstuffworks.com/environmental/energy/future-wind-turbine.htm.

National Geographic, "Geothermal Energy." www.nationalgeographic.com/environment/global-warming/geothermal-energy.

Liz Stinson, "The Future of Wind Turbines: No Blades," *Wired,* May 15, 2015. www.wired.com/2015/05/future-wind-turbines-no-blades.

Union of Concerned Scientists, "Benefits of Renewable Energy Use." www.ucsusa.org/clean-energy/renewable-energy/public-benefits-of-renewable-power.

Windustry, "History and Future of Wind Energy." www.windustry.org/history_future_of_wind_energy.

INDEX

PICTURE CREDITS

ABOUT THE AUTHOR

In addition to his numerous acclaimed volumes on ancient civilizations, historian Don Nardo has published several studies of scientific discoveries and phenomena, including *Climate Change, Polar Explorations, Volcanoes,* and award-winning books on astronomy and space exploration. Nardo also composes and arranges orchestral music. He lives with his wife, Christine, in Massachusetts.

DATE DUE

			PRINTED IN U.S.A.